THE GARAGE SALE
HOW-TO GUIDE

Everything You Need To Know
To Hold A Successful Garage Sale

By Cindy Sabulis

ISBN-13: 978-1-5300-6721-3

Table of Contents

Introduction

How much you put into planning a garage sale, along with a little luck, can mean the difference between a sale that's successful and one that's a failure. While luck, like good weather, isn't always something you can control, there are plenty of things you can do for your sale to help make that good luck happen. In this book, you'll learn what you need to do before and during a sale to help ensure it is a success. From years of experience and through trial and error I've learned what is needed to pull off a successful sale and what things to avoid. I'm going to share the methods and tricks I've learned so you don't have to go through years of on-the-job training like I did.

Whether your motivation in holding a sale is to clear out all the excess junk in your basement or garage, or whether it's to make some extra money, this book will help guide you to success.

Before planning any kind of sale, you should check to see what is allowed or not allowed in your town or community. Some towns require a permit to hold any kind of sale. Some towns only allow you to hold one or two sales per year. Some gated communities or condo associations don't allow any sales, some only allow a one day sale once a year. When it comes to hanging signs for your sale, some towns won't permit you to put up any signs. Some allow signs only for the weekend of the sale and then they must be removed or the person who posted them can be fined. Some towns allow signs at ground level, but not on any poles.

Do a bit of investigating first to find out what is permitted and not permitted before holding your sale. You don't want any surprises like getting hit with a $100 fine for hanging signs where they aren't allowed, or being asked to shut your sale down when you have several dozen people in your yard wanting to buy your stuff. This doesn't happen often, but it could.

Once you know what is or isn't allowed in your town or community you can start planning your ultra-successful garage sale.

Chapter 1: Deciding
What, Where, When

What Kind of Sale

Originally the term *yard sale* indicated the sale was held in a yard and a *garage sale* was held in a garage, but these days it doesn't seem to matter where you hold it, the terms are used interchangeably. The term *tag sale* is commonly used instead of yard or garage sale in selected areas, especially eastern parts of the country. The term came from the idea that you put tags on items for sale—not that you are selling tags as one of my friends believed years ago. The term *tag sale* is most common where I live, but some parts of the U.S. rarely or never use the term and find it too foreign. For the benefit of those who never say *tag sale*, I'll stick to using the terms *garage sale* or *yard sale* in this book.

If you decide to call your sale a moving sale, it implies you are moving out of the location where you are holding the sale and you'll have lots of stuff that you'll be getting rid of. Buyers will be hoping for bargain prices at moving sales because they know the seller has to unload it all. Moving sales are held in any location you choose, whether it be your garage, your yard, or inside your house.

Estate sales are usually held if someone has passed away and everything inside their house or apartment is for sale. However, an estate sale can also be held if someone is still living, but is getting rid of a large chunk of their possessions for some reason (foreclosure on their house, relocating, combining two households into one, etc.). An estate sale usually includes an entire household full of stuff—from furniture to clothing, and everything in between.

More times than not, estate sales are held inside a house or apartment, although some estate sales are held outdoors, often under tents in case of rain. Sometimes people who are cleaning out a house of a relative who passed away try to sell a couple of tables worth of stuff in a driveway and call it an estate sale. From the standpoint of garage salers, this wouldn't be considered an estate sale. Yes, someone passed away, and yes, the family is cleaning out their estate, but a couple of tables of merchandise doesn't exactly make it an estate sale. If you're going to call something an estate sale, make sure you deliver the goods or you'll have a lot of disappointed customers. If you're only selling a few tables worth of items, whether indoors, or in the yard, it would be better to call it an *indoor sale or a yard sale* rather than an estate sale. If you're cleaning out your own house and are opening it up to buyers, even though no one died, it's okay to call it an estate sale.

Where to Hold It

Sales held in a yard or driveway get the most visibility from people driving by, but if you have a garage that has enough free space to set up tables, a basement with easy access for people to enter, or a large porch that is enclosed or has an overhang, you can hold your sale rain or shine. The benefit of holding your sale in a basement, a garage, or in an enclosed porch is that you can set up your sale several days (or weeks) in advance, saving yourself a lot of time and work setting up the day of the sale. Keep in mind if you hold your sale inside, you will need some kind of attention-getter outside, as well as signs directing people right to the entrance where you're having it.

Most people prefer to hold garage or yard sales at their own house rather than cart all their stuff somewhere else to try to sell it. Carting everything to another location is a lot of work, but there are times when it's more beneficial to hold your sale somewhere other than your own home.

If you live on a road where it's difficult for cars to park, that might be a reason to hold your sale somewhere else. If people can't find a place to park, many will end up driving off without stopping.

If you live in a community that doesn't allow sales, or in a small condo or apartment with no place to hold a sale, holding a sale offsite might be your only option.

If you live miles from a town deep in the back woods where you see more bears than cars--that might not be the best location to hold a garage or yard sale. All the work required for a sale won't pay off if you only get one or two customers because you're far from civilization. There are exceptions, but the majority of garage salers will head towards the area where there are lots of sales being held rather than drive miles to go to a single sale. Collectors might be willing to make that drive if you have something special they want, say lots of signed art work by in-demand artists or a vintage toy collection. In instances like those, the key is to do a lot of work to bring those customers to you--that includes advertising it right.

If you have a family member or a friend who lives in a high traffic area or lives on a street that is easily accessible with plenty of parking, why not hook up with them and hold a double-sized sale at their place? If a friend has a large garage where you can set things up early and you don't, that's a good reason to move the sale to his or her place instead of holding it at yours.

If you have stuff located in a storage unit and you need to get rid of it all, many of these places won't allow you to hold a sale on their premises. In cases like this, you might need to cart all your stuff somewhere else to sell it.

It's no big secret that location can make or break your sale. While ideally having your sale where all your stuff is located is easier than carting it to another location, in some instances it is necessary, and in other instances it could pay off in much higher sales.

Best Seasons For Sales

Where I live, spring and fall are usually the best seasons to hold a garage sale. Summers are okay too. However, in the summer many people go on vacation and aren't out garage saling so you might lose a lot of potential buyers. Even though I've held sales in July and August and done okay, I do better April through June and September and October. I've held sales as early as March and as late as mid-November. For other areas of the country, the months and seasons that work best for sales might be different.

If you live where a lot of tourists swarm your town every summer, summers could be the ideal garage sale times for you. If you live in a warm climate area, any time of the year might be fine for a sale. In colder climates, stick to April-October and avoid planning a sale for the months when snow is a possibility.

I find not as many yard salers go out if the weather is too hot or too humid, or they'll only be out in the early morning and the rest of the day you'll be sitting around sweating it out without any customers. For this reason, I try to avoid July or August for holding a sale. I've run sales both in March and November which were successful dollar wise, and I believe part of the reason was because there were hardly any other sales in the area to choose from so buyers flocked to mine. This could have gone the other way too—not as many buyers out garage saling that time of year where I live, but the amount of advertising I did helped bring in people. During my cold weather sales, I found people stayed longer because they weren't in a hurry to get to other sales since there weren't many around. The downside was I had to contend with cold temperatures all day long. Depending on the climate

14

where you live, you might be able to hold a sale any month of the year--or you might only have a small window of time in which to hold it.

Holding a sale on a holiday weekend is tricky. Sometimes it can work for you or against you, depending on many factors. I can't tell you whether or not it's a good idea, but I can tell you some of the things to take into account before deciding if you want to try your luck holding a sale during a holiday weekend. First off, the competition for other sales will probably be less because a lot of people don't want to be bogged down on a holiday doing a sale. If there aren't many sales in the area that weekend, you'll stand a good chance of having hungry shoppers come to yours. On the flip side of that, not as many people will be out shopping because of holiday weekend travel plans, picnics, parades, family get togethers, etc. Some shoppers don't bother going out on holiday weekends because there aren't as many sales so they feel it's not worth going for only a few.

Sometimes having a sale on a three-day weekend is fine, but holding it on a Monday holiday probably won't bring in a lot of sales. If there are a lot of activities in your area going on for the holiday, you'll be competing with them. However, if there happens to be a big event like a parade and the parade route is close to your house, you may be able to capitalize on all the foot and car traffic to bring in buyers.

As a norm, I don't like having sales on holiday weekends, however, some friends of mine held a yard sale on Good Friday and they were jammed with shoppers all day. Their sale was located right off a busy street with lots of car traffic and lots of shopping establishments, so a few signs posted on that main street helped them to capitalize on the busy holiday traffic. I also helped a friend with a two-day sale on Friday and Saturday of Columbus Day weekend and we did amazing. The location of the sale had a lot of foot traffic—people walking by all day long, and many of them stopped to shop. Both these times I was skeptical about whether or not people would come out for the sales on a holiday weekend, but because both sales were held in high traffic areas they were successful.

How Long and What Day(s)

For a yard, garage or moving sale, holding your sale for one to three days is the norm. The more stuff you have, the better the chances of getting rid of it if you have your sale for more than one day. If you don't have too much stuff to sell, a one-day sale may be all you'll need. A two- or three-day sale tends to get rid of more things and makes more money than a one-day sale. If you are holding an indoor estate sale, you can get away with having a sale for up to a week, although expect the number of people who come to drop each day you hold it.

In some areas, Thursdays and Fridays are the best days to hold yard sales. Other areas, Fridays and Saturdays are best. Still others, Saturday and Sunday are best. Where I live, Sunday sales are usually slow in terms of the number of people who go out looking for sales that day. However, enough people have stopped and brought things at my Sunday sales to make it worthwhile for me to use it as a final sale day. If you live close to a flea market that is open on Sunday and they get a large following, then a Sunday sale may work great for you. Ditto, if you live close to a church with a large congregation. If you think you'll be able to lure those church goers to your sale at the end of their services, then absolutely, give it a go.

It's best to go with the norm for your area—that is, the days when the most people will be out looking for sales, whether it's Thursdays, Fridays, Saturdays or Sundays. You might get lucky if you try going against the norm and hold your sale on a day when no one else does, but it's a gamble. On one hand maybe every garage saler will flock to your sale because it's the only one being held on a Tuesday anywhere else in your town. On the other hand, most garage salers won't think to look for a sale on Tuesday so won't show. You'll have to decide if it's worth taking the chance.

Setting the Date

In the "old" days with print advertising you had to decide early when to have your sale and then stick to that date. That meant if monsoon season suddenly struck, you were stuck holding your sale that weekend in the rain or risk diehard garage salers knocking on your door at 6am looking for the sale you cancelled. With digital advertising, you don't have to lock into a date as early as you used to. The exception to this are estate sales where you should set a date and stick with it. For yard or garage sales, there is more flexibility of not committing to a date so early. Unless you choose to use a lot of print advertising in local newspapers, you don't have to decide until a few days before the sale whether or not it's a go. That being said, you should still be getting ready for the sale—whether it's this week or a month away.

JUNE

SUNDAY	MONDAY	TUESDAY	WEDNESDAY	THURSDAY	FRIDAY	SATURDAY
-Borrow tables -Compose ads - Make signs	1	2	3	4	5	
6	7	8	9	10	11	12
13	14	15	16	17	18	19 Garage Sale
20	21	22	23	24	25	26
27	28	29	30			

If you have the luxury of a garage or covered area where you can hold your sale rain or shine, you can pick a date and stick to it, however, I find rainy sales rarely make what sunny sales make. For that reason, I try not to hold sales if the weather forecast is calling for anything more than 20% chance of rain.

If you're like me and want to do whatever you can to try to avoid a rainy weekend for your sale, pick two or three potential weekends when you can hold it. When the first date gets close, check the weather before deciding if it's a go or no-go for the sale that weekend. If it looks like rain, you might want to hold off until your second choice weekend. While you're waiting to see what the weather will do, you should still be preparing for your sale. If you have a garage where the sale will be held, start carting things out to it and if possible, start setting up. If you don't have a garage where you can start setting up, at least make sure all your merchandise is priced. Once you see the weather predictions for the upcoming weekend and you've decided it's a go for your sale, that's when you should start an aggressive online advertising campaign.

Piggybacking Other Events

Like everything else, holding your sale on the same day as another nearby event can either work for or against you, so you'll have to weigh the pros and cons to decide if you should do it. If it's a similar event such as a flea market right down the street, you might do well if you can lure customers from the flea market over to your sale. However, you might find after they've wandered around for hours at a flea market, they aren't in a hurry to buy any more stuff by the time they get to your sale.

If the other event you want to piggyback is totally different than yours, say a music fest, or a fair of some kind, the people going to it might be more focused on the other activity than stopping at your sale. If they do stop, it might be just for a quick look before going to the other event, or after they've already spent all their money there.

If the other event will be drawing a good-size crowd, you can benefit from it for your own sale if you work hard enough. Follow the advertising and sign making tips I provide in this guide to help bring people to your sale. Don't skimp on advertising because you think you'll get enough traffic from the other event if you just hang a sign or two near it. Do plenty of your own advertising so that yard salers who might be going to the other event will know in advance you'll be selling stuff right down the street. You also want to get word out about your sale to those yard sale people who weren't planning to go to the other event, so advertise the same way you would if there wasn't an event going on nearby.

Be sure to put out something that will attract attention so people driving by on their way to the other event will notice your sale. If your sale isn't visible from the street where all the traffic is, put something there that will catch their eye and bring the crowds to you, like a large garage sale sign with a bright red arrow pointing to your sale and some balloons tied to it.

If possible, open your sale earlier than the other event and stay open until after they close. If they open at 9am, you should open at 7 or 8am so customers will come to you first while they still have money in their pocket. I once conducted a sale right down the street from a Renaissance Faire and even though we had a steady stream of Renaissance Faire goers stopping at our sale all day long, the hour before the faire opened was when we had the most "lords and ladies" opening their money pouches to buy something. If you can stay open later than the other event, you might be able to snag people as they head home, including some of the workers after they close up the place. Waiting it out until the end of the other event could result in a few late day sales for you.

If you decide the pros outweigh the cons and you're going to go ahead and piggyback a nearby event with your sale, don't skimp on the advertising, open up earlier than they do, and stay open later to increase your chances for success.

Chapter 2: Preparation

Gather Merchandise

Weeks, even months, prior to your sale, start stockpiling things you want to get rid of. If possible, store everything you want to sell in a single location like a corner in your basement or garage. As you find things around the house that you no longer need, put them in the garage sale location. The smaller items should go in boxes, the larger stuff should be covered to keep dust or garage grime from settling on it. For things you don't want to move until the day of the sale such as large pieces of furniture or items you might still be using but want to get rid of, keep a running list of them. In all the chaos that happens the morning of the sale you don't want to forget to put out a big item you were hoping to get rid of. Checking your list of things to sell that morning will help ensure you don't forget anything.

In the weeks leading up to your sale do as much decluttering as you can in each room in your home. Anything you no longer need should be placed with the stuff for your sale or noted on your sales list.

What to Sell at Your Sale

Old, outdated clothing, toys that aren't complete, furniture that's not in the best shape, half bottles of perfume, partly used nail polish, half bottles of cleaning products, old pet supplies, house plants you are tired of watering—you name it, it can be sold at your garage sale—providing it is legal, of course. Obviously, you can't sell things like firearms, alcohol, tobacco, or drugs at your sale, but most items around your house are fair game.

Don't assume no one will want something because you think it's a piece of junk. Before discarding anything you think isn't sales-worthy, try selling it. There is no guarantee the buyer who wants it will come to your garage sale, but it's worth a shot. If it doesn't sell, you can donate or toss it after the sale, but at least try to sell an item before dismissing the idea that no one will want it.

Jewelry and tools are always hot sellers in my area. Other popular items are furniture, baby items, and clothing. While popular, these items are hit or miss with the people looking for them—what you have might not be the right size, the right style, or even the right price for a buyer. At one sale you might sell a lot of children's toys. The next sale you hold, maybe no toys will sell. Every sale is different. You never know what people who come to your sale are looking for, so put out everything you'd like to get rid of and hope it's right for the people who show up.

In order to increase the money you bring in at your garage sale, you should try to sell several big ticket items. Selling a lot of $1 items is fine—I've sold many small items at my garage sales for 50 cents to $1.00 and they have added up at the end of the day, but selling a dozen items that are priced at $10 and $20 each, or just two items priced at $100 each add up a lot faster.

Furniture is usually a big ticket item and is popular with garage salers. If it's priced reasonably, is in good shape, and is appealing to a number of people it will usually find a new home. Things like a swing set, a baby stroller, and a high chair are all things that garage salers might be looking for, and if you sell any of them, your sales income can take a quick jump. Small items at your sale priced under $1.00 are great to have, but also try to have many $5, $10, and $20+ items as well, and several items that are priced over $50 if you want to make the jump from *just-okay* to *pretty-decent* sales totals.

Clean Before Selling

You want to get the best possible price you can for your stuff, so making it look nice will help you do that. Before selling anything that is dirty, dusty, or covered in cobwebs, spruce it up with a quick cleaning and you can expect to get more for it than if you leave it as is. Some bargain hunters don't care if something is dirty—as long as it is priced cheap, but common household items always sell better if they are clean. If you want to get the best price for something, clean it first.

Check for Hidden Items

I've purchased purses and backpacks at garage sales and found everything from makeup to money to unexpired credit cards hidden inside. I once found an envelope containing $250 in cash tucked inside a donated book that I purchased for 25 cents at a firemen's fund raising sale. The $250 was immediately turned over to the firemen after I discovered it, but most people if they buy something of yours with money inside wouldn't do the same.

At our local library where I volunteer we often get donations of used books for our book sales with things stashed in them, including a bunch of foreign dollar bills from WWII, a handful of old school report cards from the 1930s, and old family photos just to name a few. I know someone who sold a nightstand that belonged to their grandmother that had cash stashed behind the drawer of the nightstand. Luckily, the person who bought the nightstand was an acquaintance with a conscience and brought the money back. Of course, the buyer could have kept it and no one would have been the wiser about it.

I've heard dozens of stories about people finding gift cards, cash, jewelry, and all kinds of hidden treasures inside something they purchased at a sale. Most people probably never miss whatever was hidden inside something that was sold or donated, but you don't want to be one of those people. Before selling or donating anything, check it completely for hidden or forgotten items. All pockets of clothing, coats, purses, wallets, suitcases, and backpacks should be thoroughly checked. The pages of all books should be flipped through. If you're selling furniture like dressers, desks, end tables, or nightstands, pull out all the drawers completely and look behind them and underneath them, as well as underneath the furniture itself in case the original owner taped an envelope with valuables to the bottom.

Check under cushions and in the recesses of couches and recliners. Check, double check, and triple check everything you are selling that might have a hidden spot where treasures could have fallen or been stashed, then have someone else check them as well. Selling a jacket for $2 that has a $20 bill inside the pocket isn't very profitable. Selling the only known picture of your great grandmother that was tucked inside a book is a loss that cannot be measured.

Price Everything

You know how frustrating it is to go in a store and see something you want to buy, but there's no price on it and the only salesperson to ask is busy at the cash register with a long line of customers waiting to be checked out? It's just as frustrating for shoppers when that sort of thing happens at a garage sale. Make sure your customers see the prices of everything you're selling. If you're helping one customer, other customers won't want to hang around just to find out a price on something. Some people take the attitude "it's probably too expensive anyway" and leave without asking or they don't want it bad enough to waste their time waiting around to find out the price. Some customers are shy about asking the prices for everything that interests them.

I've heard from many people who go to garage sales that unless they find an item they are dying for, they won't buy anything at a sale if nothing is marked. While not everyone feels this way, enough people do that you're going to lose sales if you don't price your stuff. It takes a lot of time to price everything you're selling, but it's to your benefit as well as to your customers to do so. Some people may not be in the market for a particular item, but if they see it marked at a bargain price, they'll buy it because it's a good deal—not necessarily because they were dying to own it. Those "nothing" items you're selling--the little things that you think no one will want, often sell if they are priced low. Things like leftover party hats from your toddler's last birthday party, a deck of cards, a half-used pad of paper--if they have no price on them, they often don't sell. If you have them marked only 10 cents, they are more likely to go home with someone who can't resist a bargain.

To stress this important point again because it can help sell your stuff and help make your sale successful—*price your merchandise.*

One shortcut to pricing items is to use price lists. A sign listing stuffed animals could say, "Large...$1.00 each. Medium...50 cents each. Small...25 cents each." For clothing, a sign listing how much you are asking for pants, shirts, jackets, sweaters, dresses, etc. can be hung near the clothes. If you have a lot of books, it's much simpler if you can put up a sign making all hardcover books one price and softcover another rather than trying to price individual books. Some people like to use color coded price stickers to simplify things. Anything with a yellow sticker is one price, with a blue sticker another price, pink another...etc. As a customer, I find this system inconvenient because I'm constantly glancing at the sticker-colored price list to find out how much every item I am interested in costs. While inconvenient for shoppers like myself who can't remember that the pink stickers mean $1 and the blue stickers mean a quarter, it does simplify the task of pricing a lot of items.

If you have several items that you can price the same, put them in a box and write large and legibly on the front of the box "50 cents each" or whatever price you want for them. Marking a whole box of stuff with one sign on it is easier than marking everything in the box individually. The risk of putting things in one box with a single price is people might bring you things from the $1.00 box and claim they got out of the 25 cent box. If you don't care, no big deal. If you do care, then you're better off sticking a price tag on every item in the box. Under no circumstances should you have sharp items or anything breakable in a box that people will be digging through. If you have a whole collection of ceramic figurines in a box with a "$1.00 each" half those figurines will get chipped or broken as people rifle through them. Be mindful about what you leave in boxes vs. what needs to be on a table.

Setting Prices

How do you determine what price to put on an item? This is always tricky. It would help if you went to a few sales prior to holding your own to determine what others ask for similar items. While copying other sellers' prices doesn't always insure you're pricing something right on the mark, at least it gives you a ballpark figure. People who have garage sales but have never actually gone to any themselves often make the mistake of pricing things too high or too low. Go to a few sales in your area to get an idea what the asking price of things are--plus it will give you some ideas on how to display things for your own sale.

If you can't go to any sales on a weekend, at least check out the local thrift shops to see what they are asking for common items such as books, clothing, furniture, baby items, etc. Use that only as a guide, not as positive proof you'll get those prices because some of the higher-priced thrift shops can have something for months before it sells. You only have days to sell your stuff so it should be priced to sell quickly.

If you are selling something that you know could be valuable but don't know what to ask for it, check out ending auctions on eBay to see if the same item has sold there, then price your item about 25-50% lower than the average eBay selling price for it. Research values by using only the sold prices on eBay, not current or unsold auctions. Be realistic when pricing things you've researched on eBay--you most likely won't get eBay prices at your yard sale, and trying to justify your high price on something by saying, "It sells high on eBay" just turns bargain hunters off. If you want high eBay prices for something, put it on eBay. If you don't have the ambition to do the work it takes to sell it on eBay, than you should sell it for a much lower price—probably to someone who will end up putting it on eBay.

Below is a sample price list of what some common yard sale items might sell for. It is just a guide to get you started. Many different factors come into play when pricing anything. The quality, the condition, how much demand there is for it, and your location all play a part in how high or how low you should price an item. If you want to get rid of things, price them at yard sale prices—not eBay or Amazon prices.

Books and Media
Children's Books: 25¢-$1
Adult Paperbacks (older or smaller size): 25¢-50¢
Adult Paperbacks (more current titles/larger size paperbacks): 50¢-$1
Adult Hardcover: 50¢-$2
DVDs: $1-$3 ($10-$15 if a whole series)
Music CDs: $1-$3
LP Vinyl Record Albums: 50¢-$2

Clothing (Adults/Teens)
Jeans: $1-$5

T-shirts: 50¢-$1

Shirts: $1-$4

Sweatshirts: 50¢-$2

Sweaters: $2-$3

Dresses: $2-$5 and up depending on how fancy

Shoes: $1-$5

Baby Clothing: 25¢-$3

Children's Clothing: 25¢-$3

Girl's Specialty Dresses or Boy's Dress Suits: $5-$15

Costume Jewelry (lower end stuff): 50¢-$5

Higher-End Jewelry: you're better off getting appraised before selling

Toys and Games

Board Games: 25¢-$2

Action Figures/Dolls: 10¢-$2

Stuffed Animals: 25¢-$2

Video Games: $1-$20 (depending on age, popularity, and collectibility)

Kitchen Items

Glasses, Cups: 25¢-$1

Bowls: 25¢-$1

Plates: $1 each

Dishes (Sets): $5-$50

Pots and Pans: $1-$4

Microwaves: $5-$20

Small Appliances: $3-$20

Large Appliances: $30-$300

Electronics

Radio: $1-$3

Old Computers: $5-$45 (depending on how current)

TV: $5-$100 (depending on how current)

DVD Players: $20-$25

Tools

Hand Tools (hammer, screwdriver, etc.): $1-$3

Electric Sander: $5-$15

Electric Drill: $5-$15

Garden supplies:

Rakes: $1-$2

Shovels: $1-$3

Weed Trimmer: $10-$20

Hedge Trimmer: $5-$10

Lawn Mower: $25-$100

Household Items

Recliners: $25-$100

Couches: $25-$300

Desks: $15-$200

Dressers: $15-$200

Dining Room Table & Chairs: $30-$400

Bed Frames: $25-$200 (some states don't allow you to sell used mattresses, so check before selling).

Linens and Bedding: $2-$15

Again, these prices are just a guide. One dress might be worth only $1 to bargain hunters, while another designer name, fancy one you might be able to get $25. Furniture prices fluctuate depending on the quality, condition, how old it is, as well as the original cost. An old beat up bed you'll be lucky to get $20 for, while a fancy new one or an antique bed you might be able to sell for $1,000. If your furniture is only a couple years old and still in good shape, a fair yard sale price is probably about ½ the original cost.

You might want to consider selling some of your higher priced items like furniture on Craigslist prior to your sale. Buyers are willing to pay more for something listed on Craigslist than at a yard sale. Things like designer clothing may do significantly better selling in a consignment shop then at your yard sale, so you might want to consign them rather than trying to sell them at your sale. If you don't mind selling stuff in multiple ways, it could bring you more money. If it's more about getting rid of stuff than making money, than by all means put everything out at your yard sale. Price them low and watch them go.

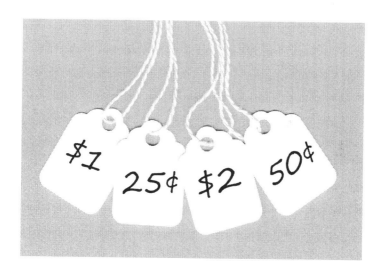

Chapter 3: Advertising

The Importance of Advertising

I can't stress this enough—*you have to advertise your sale*. A lot. How much advertising you do for your sale can mean the difference of making $50 or making $2,000.

Ideally, you should advertise in many different venues, and in the case of online advertising, multiple times. The more places you advertise, the more people will see it. If you have a local paper with a big circulation, it might be worth your while to pay for an ad in it. Many papers will place their print ads online as well, so you'll get double the exposure, but sometimes paying for only an online ad with a paper and not the print part might be all you need. Every area is different, so you'll need to do a little homework and ask around to see where most garage salers in your area look to find garage sales.

I'm a big online advertiser. When I hold a sale, I'll spend days on my computer promoting it with online ads and pictures. Some online places charge, but there are plenty of free sites all over the internet where you can advertise your upcoming sale. The free places are the ones I use most frequently.

Advertising on Craigslist

One of the best online places to advertise garage sales is Craigslist, and the best part is it's free. You're allowed to post up to 24 pictures with each ad. Adding lots of photos of the stuff you are selling at your sale will help get people excited about coming to it. If you don't already have a Craigslist account and you're planning to have a garage sale at some point, sign up for Craigslist now.

If you live in a large city, your Craigslist ad can quickly get lost among the hundreds of other ads that are posted every day for your area. To help ensure people in your area see yours, place one ad under the garage sale category early in the week, and a second revised one later in the week. You'll have a better chance of people seeing at least one of your ads if you post them on different days. When I say put a "revised" ad, I mean it can't be the same ad you put on earlier in the week. Craigslist's spam filter won't allow you to have two identical ads running, so if you decide to do two, make sure your second ad is different enough from the first to fall under the spam filter radar. If you live in a less populated area, one listing under the garage sale category of your local Craigslist will probably be enough unless you happen to pick the same weekend that everyone else has selected to hold garage sales and Craigslist is being flooded with ads. In that case, you might want to consider putting up a second garage sale ad.

For the ad(s) you run in the garage sale section of Craigslist, be sure to add plenty of photos of what you are selling in order to get people interested in coming. The more stuff potential customers see for sale in your ad, the more likely they'll pick your sale to attend over others. If you can set up at least a small portion of your sale early in the week (on a porch or in a garage), take photos of those sale items from many different angles and post the best picture as the leading picture for your Craigslist ad. That first picture will be the picture that will appear in Craigslist's gallery view. A picture filled with lots of stuff to look at will get more people to click on it in Craigslist's gallery view than an ad with a picture of a single item like a refrigerator or a computer. You'll still want to take a picture of the refrigerator or computer—just use them as secondary photos. Anything large or big ticket that you are especially interested in getting rid of such as furniture or a boat should have its own photo in your Craigslist ad. As your sale gets closer, if you add more stuff to your setup or sales pile, take more photos and add them to your Craigslist ads. You can delete any photo you previously added if need be and replace it with newer, improved photos that better show off your merchandise.

The category of garage sales on Craigslist is where you'll definitely want to place an ad, but you should also place ads in as many other Craigslist categories as are relevant to your sale. For instance, if you'll be selling a lot of books at your garage sale, put an ad under the books/for sale category telling the Craigslist world that tons of books on all subjects will be available at your garage sale. If you'll be selling a lot of children's items, put an ad under the baby and kid/for sale category. If you have a lot of vinyl records to sell, put an ad under CD/DVD/VHS/for sale. Furniture? Definitely list what you have in the furniture/for sale category on Craigslist. With all these individual ads include photos, and say that the items will be available at your garage sale and include the date(s), time, and address.

By advertising your sale in multiple categories, you'll increase the odds that different people will see them, thus increasing the odds that more people will come to your sale. As mentioned above, Craigslist's spam filters won't allow you put the exact same ad twice, even in different categories. However, you are allowed to advertise similar ads in different categories as long as Craigslist spam filters don't think you are trying to spam the system or individuals who have nothing better to do don't flag your ads as spam.

If you live near two overlapping Craigslist regions, place garage sale ads in both of them. Again, you have to make sure the two ads are different enough from each other to satisfy Craigslist. Revise your ads by changing the wording around, adding a few extra sentences, and deleting some words. In addition to revising the body of the ad, you also need to revise the title. Revise it enough so that even though you are advertising the same thing, you have two different ads that will fall under the radar of Craigslist spam filters.

In addition to not allowing the same ad to be posted in multiple categories, Craigslist has some other rules that if you break them, your ad could be flagged for deletion. Some of these rules may change after this is published, but I'll mention a few just to give you an idea of what you might need to watch out for.

Anyone using Craigslist can flag an ad—it's supposed to be a self-policing system, and of course, it doesn't always work as it should. If your ad gets pulled for no apparent reason you can figure out, try posting a new ad exactly like it 24 hours later and see if it stays there. Some people flag ads because they feel it doesn't belong in the category it's posted in, but sometimes mean-spirited people flag ads just because they feel like it. Some people flag ads because they don't want the competition. Sometimes Craigslist will automatically delete something if their robot thinks you broke one of their rules. If you get an e-mail saying your ad was deleted for being in the wrong category, for keyword spamming (using too many keywords in order to have your ad show up in lots of searches), or you already posted that same ad in another category, rectify it and repost. Craigslist also limits you to three posts at a time and if you try to post more you'll get a message saying "you're posting too fast." You'll have to wait a few minutes before you can post again.

There are so many ads placed on Craigslist every day it's easy for your ads to get buried quickly. It helps to stagger your ads. Do a few ads each day or some in the morning and some in the evening so that your ads aren't all at the top of the listing one day, then all at the bottom the next day.

Make your title enticing enough so people will want to click on it. Titling your ad simply "Garage Sale" will get lost in lots of other postings that say the same thing. Instead try something like, "Yard Sale: Tons of Furniture, Collectibles, Vintage Items, Jewelry + More." A title like that will stand out from the plain vanilla titles and will more likely get people to click on your ad.

Don't skimp on the length of your title--use as many characters as Craigslist allows. Try not to waste space using commas or other punctuation unless you have one or two spaces left over that you can't use for something better. Writing your titles all in caps sometimes works to make your ad more visible if someone is viewing Craigslist as word listings, but only if all the other titles around yours are in lower case. If everyone types their titles all in caps, your ad will get lost with all the others, plus seeing all those caps gets annoying to most people. Caps may occasionally be okay in your title, but whatever you do, don't use all caps in the body of your ad.

In the body of your ad list all the big items you are selling as well as all the expensive items, anything you have a lot of, and anything you think is interesting. Simply putting "Something for everyone" says nothing to buyers. However typing up a list of things will entice more buyers who are looking for specific items on your sales list as well as buyers who figure you might have other good stuff too (even if they didn't see anything they wanted on your list). More is better when it comes to listing stuff, but whatever you do, don't clump them all together in one paragraph that is difficult to read. It's much better to place every item on a separate line so that potential buyers can scan your list easily. Making your list with bullets makes it neater and even easier to read.

Sample Craigslist Ads

Here are some sample ads that will help yours stand out from the others.

(Title) Giant Sale: 20 years of accumulation collectibles children's stuff
(Body) Having a blowout yard sale featuring 20 years of accumulation. Just some of the items to be sold include:

- Mid-century mod dining room table
- Vintage end tables for repurpose/restoration
- Thomas Playmate duel keyboard organ with bench
- Vintage camera collection as well as newer 35mm cameras and lenses
- Over 500 LP record albums
- Art Deco smoking stand ashtray w/cigar lighter
- Sewing machine with mid-century cabinet
- Vintage chain saw
- Set of antique lamps
- Collection of old snow globes from the Disney Store
- Lots of household items
- Hordes of craft supplies
- Fisher Price bounce house
- High chair barely used
- Children's books
- Girls' clothing size 6 through 12
- Toys
- Lots of eBay-worthy items priced to sell
- Lots of 25 cent-$1.00 items

Sale will be held on *(date/time)* at *(address)*

An ad like the one above is more likely to get people to come than an ad that just says, "Yard Sale. Something for everyone."

If you have lots of a particular item, post a separate ad for it in a different Craigslist's category. For example, if you have a lot of craft items, write up an ad like the one below to put under the arts and crafts/for sale section of Craigslist:

(Title) Lots of Crafts Needlework Knitting Crocheting Supplies
(Body) Selling lots of craft and needlework supplies at our yard sale this coming weekend. Most items priced at 25 cents up to $2.00. We have tons of craft magazines, knitting needles, crochet hooks, ribbon, trim, craft kits, craft booklets, some fabric, lots of bits and pieces for craft or sewing projects. Items are available for viewing only during the sale. Sale will be held at *(address)* on *(date and time)*.

Do you have lots of video games or a couple of video systems you're selling? Post an ad in the video gaming/for sale section of Craigslist:

(Title) 70+ Video Games, 5 systems Super Nintendo N64 GameCube PS3 PSP

(Body) Selling over 70 video games and 5 different gaming systems at our yard sale this coming weekend. We have Super Nintendo, N64, GameCube, PS3, PSP systems and accessories and games. Most games priced $1-$5. All games in their original boxes with booklets. Items available only at our yard sale on *(date and time)* at *(address)*. No early buyers please.

With every ad, include pictures. As of this writing, you can put up to 24 pictures in each Craigslist ad. In every ad, put your most enticing picture as your first one. Anyone viewing Craigslist in gallery format will see only that first picture before they click on your ad, so you'll want the best picture to entice them to click on it to see more. Make that gallery picture a good one. For each ad posted under the various categories include a few photos of those things you're specifically promoting in the ad like all your video games or all your boxes of crafting supplies first, but you can also post some pictures of your other garage sale stuff in those ads to help entice additional viewers to come to your sale.

Advertising on Facebook

Facebook is another excellent place for free advertising. Several weeks (or even months) before you have your sale start joining some of the local yard sale groups or buy/sell groups on Facebook. There could be many selling groups in your area you might not be aware of where you could advertise your sale. Try searching Facebook for "Yard Sale," "Garage Sale," "Tag Sale," "Buy Sell" or "For Sale" followed by the name of every town near you to find them all. After you searched and joined some of these groups, Facebook will probably start suggesting similar groups when you're logged in.

Join as many local selling groups as you can and learn what their rules are before posting. I once got kicked out of a Facebook group for posting a photo of some baby items that were being sold at our neighborhood yard sale by one family, not realizing that the group was for selling items for adults only, no children's items. The administrator gave me the boot and blocked me from the group with no warning because I failed to read the rules that specified no children's items were permitted.

Some local groups might not allow the posting of yard sale notices. Check the rules before posting and if you're still not sure, it doesn't hurt to send the administrator a private message asking if it's okay to post your yard sale info. Better to ask ahead of time than to risk having your hard work of posting the information along with your photos deleted on you, or worse--getting booted out of the group altogether for not following the rules.

Some groups will only allow you to post a couple of pictures, others want you to post photos in an album if you post more than one or two. Again, learn the rules of every group where you plan to advertise your sale so you don't unknowingly break them. As long as your yard sale info is okay to post, *always* post a photo with the info. A photo will get tons more visibility both within the group and in people's newsfeeds than a few lines of typed text saying you're having a garage sale on Saturday.

Stagger your yard sale ads for different times in different Facebook groups. Many of the same people will also be members of all the different groups you'll be advertising in. Those people won't like seeing the same ad you post in ten different groups showing up in their newsfeed ten times in a row. You're better off staggering your posts to the different groups at different times. Doing it this way, you'll hit many different Facebook users who are online those different times without blatantly looking like you're spamming all the groups with your sale information. If you can change the photo(s) you use for your notice in each group, even better.

Posts get buried very quickly in Facebook groups, so it's best to post your yard sale notices the day before your sale. If you decide to post about your sale two days before to get it out of the way so you can concentrate on pricing and setting up, try to find time the evening before your sale to go back to those groups or to your activity log and bump up all the ads you posted. "Bumping" them means you try to get them to appear at the top of the group's page so people don't have to scan through all the group's posts before they see it. One way to bump your post is by making a comment on it, something like "Opening tomorrow at 8am." Lots of people bump their ads up simply by typing the word "bump" in the comment section. Some groups have rules that say, "No bumping your ads until they've been posted a week," or something similar so be careful if you bump it up this way or you might get bumped right out of the group. Adding more pictures in the comment section is a better and less obvious way of bumping it up. It's also helpful if you recruit a friend or two you have in the group to help bump the ad for you. Send them a private message asking if they would comment on your ad, and that too will move it back up to the top of the group's discussion. The more people comment on your post, the more it stays on top. Some people bump up their yard sale posts the day of their sale while they're sitting waiting for customers. Sometimes they add additional pictures, sometimes they post, "sale going on now, lots of bargains," or something similar.

If you have many local Facebook friends, be sure to also post your sale on your own Facebook wall the day before the sale. Ask your friends to help spread the word by sharing the post on their own walls too.

Other Online Advertising

Weeks in advance of your sale you should do all kinds of internet searches on phrases such as "garage sale free ads", "yard sale free ads", "tag sale free ads" and bookmark any sites where you'll be able to advertise your sale. Also, sign up ahead of time for any sites that require it, so that you don't have to deal with registering for them a few days before your sale.

I'm hesitant to list too many internet sites where you can advertise your sale, because sites come and go and a few months after I write this, the ones I tell you about might be gone and new and better ones might be out there. However, here are a few online sites (as of publication) where you can advertise, and hopefully they'll still be around by the time you read this:

- Craigslist (in multiple categories)
- Facebook (in multiple groups and on your own wall)
- Instagram
- Twitter
- Patch (any towns that are local to you)
- Gsalr.com
- Yardsalesearch.com

- Garagesalefinder.com
- Tagsellit.com

Whenever you advertise online, include pictures if possible. The more, the better. Simply having a line of text that says "something for everyone" in a post doesn't get people too excited about going to your sale. Posting a photo showing lots of merchandise is more likely to spark their interest. Posting *a lot* of pictures with *a lot* of merchandise in them will really grab their attention.

When you post your sale on social media sites, be prepared to answer questions about prices and sizes. It's sometimes a pain to measure items and answer questions the day before a sale when you already have a ton of other things to do, but take the time to answer and some of those people may come out to your sale to buy those items that interest them. Don't promise to hold anything for anyone unless it's for someone you know.

Many people I know have dealt with Craigslist or Facebook users who have promised that they definitely wanted to purchase something, but never followed through. This happens not only with individual-item sales, but with yard sales as well. A person will spot something in your yard sale pictures, contact you to ask how much, and beg you to hold it for them until they can get there. Learn from mine and many other people's experiences—if you don't know them, don't hold anything for them.

You don't want to be holding a high ticket item until noon the day of your sale for someone who promised to be there in the morning but never shows up. By holding it all morning, you've missed out on a lot of other potential buyers, and you might end up being stuck with something you could have sold to someone earlier in the day. If anyone contacts you online and asks you to hold something you're selling at your garage sale because they "definitely" want it, tell them to come 10 minutes early for it the morning of your sale. If they aren't there by the time you open your garage door to the public, the hold goes off it and its fair game. If they tell you they are working until noon or have to drop their kids off somewhere first, or some other excuse why they can't be there at the start of your sale, politely tell them to stop by any time before the end of the sale and perhaps it will still be there for sale.

Sometimes people will contact you and ask if they could come the day before your sale to buy something. I've gotten every story in the book from, "I have to go to a funeral on Friday, can I come Thursday instead?" to "I had that same (whatever) growing up but it got lost when our house burned down and it would mean the world to me if I could come tonight and buy yours." I find opening up my sale to pre-buyers is often more distracting than profitable. I've allowed people in early, only to have them take their time looking through everything in my garage, talking me down on prices of everything they are interested in, and taking up valuable time that could better be spent getting ready for the sale.

Aggressive (and often obnoxious) people aren't shy about knocking on your door the day before or e-mailing you and asking to come see your stuff early. I had one pushy dealer show up on my doorstep the day before, and even though I hadn't put my house number in my ads, she knocked on all the doors on my street until she found out who was having a sale the next day. At first I told her no, she couldn't come in to look, but she was so insistent about getting an early preview, including flashing a wad of cash in front of me saying she was ready to spend it, that I regrettably gave into her. She dug through the stuff in my garage for nearly an hour and ended up buying one small item for a couple of dollars. Lesson learned.

If someone contacts you about purchasing a specific item they saw in your yard sale ad and asks in a very respectful way if they could come out early to buy it, it's your call whether or not you want to deal with them when you're still getting ready for your sale, or whether to make them wait until the day of the sale and let them fight it out with everyone else. If it's a large ticket item that they're interested in--say a car, or a boat, or an entire room full of furniture, and they claim they can't make it the day of your sale, you might want to grab the opportunity to try to sell it. Only a limited number of buyers will be interested in those big ticket items. If they come and buy it the day before, you may risk angering someone else who comes to your sale special to see that item, but that's a risk worth taking if it means you sell the $5,000 bedroom set you were desperate to get rid of.

Advertising in Print

If you use print ads, you need to get your ad in by the publication's deadline. Once your print ad is in, you're pretty much locked into the date(s) you put for your sale. This is fine if you're going to hold your sale rain or shine. If you are going to cancel your sale in the event of rain, putting a rain date in your print ad isn't going to be enough to bring in the people the following week. Most people won't remember your sale a week later so you'll still have to put a new ad in the week of the rain date. If you're paying for the ad, it's no fun to pay for it twice, but not putting the ad the second time will affect your profits. If no rain date is planned and you're only having the sale if it doesn't rain, you should say "Rain cancels" in your ad.

When I see the commonly-used phrase "something for everyone" in print ads, I just shake my head. I've gone to many sales that have promised "something for everyone" where I haven't found anything. I'm always tempted to tell the sellers they lied in their ad. If you're paying by the word as you often are in print ads, rather than waste advertising space and money using three words that don't mean much, use that space to list three big ticket items you're selling. If placing your ad by phone, have on hand a list of items you're selling that you might use instead of that overworked phrase in case there is extra room in your ad after putting in the important details (address, date, time).

When to Advertise

If you're doing any kind of print advertising in a local newspaper or freebie papers like the Pennysaver, Thrifty Nickel, Bargain News, etc. you need to check when their ad deadline is so you can get yours in on time. You can write up your ads weeks in advance, and revise it if necessary right before submitting it.

With online ads, you can start posting a few ads early in the week of your sale, but the bulk of your online advertising should be 2-3 days before the sale, then a big burst of new advertising or bumping up some of your old ads the day and evening before the sale. If you're having a multiple-day sale, the evening after your first sale day, add a few new online ads or bump up your old ads to get more visibility for the second day.

Sign Making Tips

Don't assume placing an ad in a newspaper or on Craigslist is all you need to get people to come to your sale. You still need to advertise it by putting up signs. It's been my experience that an early burst of customers is often the result of good advertising, but the people who continue to come throughout the rest of the day do so because of all the signs I put up. No matter how much advertising you do ahead of time, you still need to hang signs if you want people to come all day long.

The more signs you put up, the more visibility you'll get--so make plenty. Most people make a bunch of signs, then go out the morning of the sale or the night before and try to figure out where to hang them. With a little advance planning you can save yourself time hanging signs if you map out where you'll be hanging them ahead of time.

Weeks before your sale, scope out all the heavily-traveled areas around your home to find the best places to place signs. If every weekend you notice a certain location near your home always has yard sale signs posted, that's probably a good place to put one of yours. Places near your home where there is a lot of foot traffic or lots of cars passing by are good places to hang signs if at all possible.

How far away from your house you should be hanging signs depends on how populated the area is where you live. If you live in a rural area, you'll want signs leading people from the higher populated area out to your home. If you live in a busy city, you may only need signs around a three- or four-block area. For suburban areas, you might need signs within a mile or two of your home.

While you're scoping out the area for where to place signs, also figure out what kind of sign you'll need for each location. Does the location have a pole where you can hang a sign? Do you need to have a freestanding sign on the ground? What size sign can be easily seen by drivers at that location? Which direction should the arrow go on the sign at each location? If you can, write down all this stuff as you discover it--good locations for signs, what kind of sign you need (freestanding or hanging), and the arrow direction. Once you have all the locations down, you now know approximately how many signs to make.

Make sure your signs are large enough to be visible without obstructing traffic. Printing pretty little signs off your computer on an 8 1/2" x 11" sheet of paper may look nice, but generally a sign that size is not easily readable from the driver's side of a car. Anything past the "Garage Sale" heading is usually too small for a driver to see.

Use sign boards that stand out. Many people use brown cardboard to make their yard sale signs because it's what they have hanging around and it's free. While using what you already have on hand is commendable and recommended whenever possible, the reality is brown cardboard doesn't stand out very effectively. Drivers won't notice your brown signs until they are right on top of it. Likewise, drivers aren't going to notice a green sign stuck on a green lawn until they drive right up to it. You want signs that really stand out so yard salers driving around looking for sales will see your sign from as far away as possible. You don't want them driving right by and not noticing your sign until it's too late to see what your sign says or for them to make a turn towards your sale.

White poster board is good for making signs, but florescent poster board is even better. Florescent color signs scream "Slow down and read me!" to drivers coming down the road. While it's okay to have one pink florescent sign and another yellow, if you keep your signs all the same color it sometimes helps people to look for all the signs of a specific color if they're following your signs to get to your sale. While poster board in any color can look appealing and attract the attention of drivers driving by, most poster board isn't sturdy enough to hold up to whatever nature throws at it. If the morning dew hits it, it will become wrinkly and limp and difficult to read before your sale is over. If one corner of your poster board sign comes loose from the wind, it might flop over the rest of the sign and make it unreadable. What I like to do is use a large piece of heavy brown (corrugated) cardboard for my foundation, and I securely staple white or florescent poster board in the center of it. The brown cardboard frames the smaller sign in the middle. By doing this, I reinforce the weight of the poster board making it less likely to get ripped or floppy, and also I get a larger sign without having to buy the larger-sized poster board.

Stores such as Home Depot, Lowes, and Staples sell white corrugated plastic garage sale signs that can hold up to rain and moisture better than cardboard. They usually come in different sizes. I advise you to buy signs that are at least 18" x 24". Some of the smaller sizes are difficult to see from a car until you are right up on them. These stores also sell small red or yellow arrow signs which many die-hard yard salers have their radar set for, but seeing the street written in the small area provided is usually challenging. If you use these smaller arrow-shaped signs, use them close to your house where the arrow leads them right to you and drivers won't have to worry about reading the street name written on it. Stores that sell corrugated plastic garage sale signs usually sell metal stakes for them as well. You'll need them if you can't hang signs on poles.

In places where there are no telephone poles to hang signs, some people make their signs on large (plain cardboard) boxes, then anchor the boxes down by placing a few heavy rocks inside. Make sure the top of your sign is towards the open top of the box, otherwise when you put your rocks in the bottom, your sign will be upside down or sideways. If you go with the box as a sign idea, either use a plain white box that will stand out, or make your sign on neon poster board then tape or staple it to the box. Again, a plain brown cardboard box tends to blend in too much with the background and drivers can easily miss it.

If you don't want to spend money on poster board (and really...who does?), it's okay to use whatever materials you have on hand to make your signs. Just be sure it is strong enough to hold up to wind, rain, or morning dew and the color stands out enough to attract the attention of drivers passing by.

Always use *permanent* marker on your signs. If you don't use permanent marker on your signs, and it happens to rain, the text on your signs will wash away. Even morning dew can wipe out any non-waterproof marker on signs. The same is true for anything you print off your computer—any moisture will make the ink run and it may end up being unreadable—even if it's only morning dew that lands on it. For this reason, I don't recommend printing your signs off your computer unless you have a printer with waterproof ink and heavy duty paper that won't wrinkle if it gets damp. Red marker stands out on a sign, but black is easier to read. If you want to use red marker, use it for the title and the arrow only, but print the rest of the text in black. Make your arrow as large as will fit on the sign so it can be seen as far away as possible by drivers.

Keep it simple. Don't put a lot of words on your sign that people passing by in cars can't read. Just the title "GARAGE SALE" or "YARD SALE" at the top in big letters, then your address, date(s), start and end times, and an arrow leading them to your sale. Nothing else.

Always put arrows on your signs. Don't assume everyone will know where your street is just from the name. Lead them to it by using arrows.

If you know where you're hanging your signs ahead of time, then you'll already know which direction you need the arrows to point. However if you haven't decided where your signs will hang, you can make some signs with the arrows going one direction, and other signs with the arrow going in the opposite direction. If you are making a two-sided sign that drivers will be able to view from two different places, be sure your arrows on either side match up so they're both going the same direction and not opposite one another. You can also make some signs with the arrow pointing upwards for straight ahead. If you're unsure which direction to make the arrow, take a permanent marker with you when you hang your signs, then draw in the arrow right there.

If you're planning to hang signs on wooden or metal poles, bring a hammer, nails, strong tape, and scissors with you. Usually utility companies who own the poles do not want any kind of signs on them, so you'll have to use discretion about what is or isn't acceptable in your area regarding hanging signs on poles. If in your town you always see signs on poles, then it might be okay for you to do so. Just keep in mind some towns or states are very strict about hanging signs on poles and might remove them, or may even fine you. If a utility company worker happens to work on the pole where your sign is, they'll most likely remove it.

Some people tape their garage sale signs to metal light poles, and depending on where you live you might get away with it. I've seen garage sale signs taped up on the poles of street or traffic signs, but this is not a good idea. People are more likely to complain to the police about a sign if it's hung in a place that is a clear violation of the law--like on a stop sign. If the police themselves see your garage sale sign hanging on a stop sign, they may come visit your house—and not with the intent to purchase stuff at your garage sale.

Some towns are sticklers for signs, and others are very lenient. I've run sales in some towns where the authorities leave notices on doors telling people they are going to be fined if they don't remove their signs off utility poles. Other towns I've seen signs left up for months and no one seemed to care. I once had a sign removed by the police the night before a sale because someone called and complained to them that it was posted on a historic green. Again, it's a good idea to check with your local authorities to see what is allowed and not allowed.

When deciding how large to make your signs, you need to be mindful of blocking drivers' views. Too big, and someone might complain to the police about it, or it could cause an accident if someone can't see around it to see oncoming traffic. Large signs that are on the ground can start flapping around if there are strong winds and can even go airborne if they're not secure enough. So, even though bigger is better to see them when it comes to signs, you still need to keep them at a manageable size. Of course, if you make them too small, drivers won't see them.

When putting up signs, as a courtesy don't block other people's yard sale signs with yours, and never hang your sign over someone else's on a pole. You wouldn't want anyone to do that to your signs, so don't do it to anyone else's. If there is an old sign on a pole and the date of the sale has come and gone, it's okay to remove it and put yours up where that one was, but if there is no room left on a pole and the other signs plastered all over it are for the same day(s) as your sale, go find another pole.

Ideally you should place your signs in high visibility areas. If you put up a sign near a busy intersection, don't put up just one sign, put up two or three signs facing different ways so cars can see your signs whatever direction they come from. When I say "busy intersection" generally I'm referring to ones in smaller towns. If you live in a large city, a busy intersection probably isn't the best place for a yard sale sign as there is too much going on there already for drivers to easily see signs, not to mention the distraction it could cause if drivers try to read it.

After your sale is over, be courteous and remove all the signs you put up. If you put your signs on utility poles with nails, it would be courteous to also remove the nails as well, so take a hammer with you when you take down your signs.

Chapter 4: Planning Ahead

If you know you're going to have a yard sale at some point, but you're not sure when, you can save yourself a lot of last minute craziness if you do as much work as possible ahead of time.

Cleaning anything you are going to sell is one thing you can do early. Pricing items is another. As you're gathering things for your sale, clean them if needed and stick a price on them before you put them in your "for sale" box. Sometimes when I price things as I go, I might inadvertently give two different prices to two similar things. For example, I might price an excellent condition shirt at $1.00, but then later may price another identical shirt in worse condition for $2.00. If I'm lucky, I'll notice this during set up, and can revise the prices. If you can price most of your things ahead of time, it will save you a lot of work when you're in crunch mode.

Making signs is another thing you can do weeks ahead of time. If you haven't locked into a date yet, put all the information for the sale on your signs except for the date and the time. Add your title ("Garage Sale" "Yard Sale" or whatever kind of sale), your address, and a directional arrow, leaving a blank space to add the date and time once you definitely decide. When your sale gets closer all that will be left to do in the sign-making department is fill in the date and times on all your signs.

Gathering small bills is another task you can do early. You're going to need lots of single-dollar bills, and some five- and ten-dollar bills to make change during your sale so you might want to start stockpiling them early. If it's easier to go to a bank the week of the sale and get low bills, that's fine, but if you start saving all your singles, fives, and a few tens in the weeks before your sale you can save yourself that trip. If you have a lot of items priced under $1.00 you'll also need nickels, dimes, and quarters. Unless you charge sales tax or have items priced at unusual amounts like $1.43, you generally don't need pennies. I like to have $100 in small bills on hand during my sale so I don't run short if a bunch of people give me $20 bills after buying a $1.00 item--and trust me, lots of people do this. Some garage sale goers tend to use the first sale where they buy something as a way to get smaller bills so they have them when they shop other sales. No matter how inexpensive the item is that they are buying, they'll give you a $20 to get the change. Be prepared for this.

Other things you can do to get ready ahead of time:

- Research and sign up for any online places where you can advertise your sale.
- Write up ads for newspapers, Craigslist, and other online places, filling in as much information as you know ahead of time. You can add more details as your sale gets closer.
- If you don't have plenty of folding tables already, ask all your friends and family if they have any you can borrow. You might need to hunt for used tables at thrift shops, yard sales, in Facebook yard sale groups, or on Craigslist.

You can also purchase new ones from a local store or from online sites.

- Create a list of e-mail addresses, and write up a small blurb to send out later notifying all your local friends of your sale.
- Take photos of large items you will be selling.
- Recruit people to help you the day of your sale.

Schedule

2-8 Weeks Before

- Gather stuff to sell
- Clean anything you are selling that is dirty
- Research selling prices of your items
- Price merchandise
- Scope out potential places to advertise
- Register on websites where you plan to advertise
- Start making signs
- Compose ads
- Compile e-mail addresses and compose e-mail regarding sale to send to local friends/family
- Take photos of items for sale
- Recruit friends/family to help

All these things can be done the week before your sale, but the earlier you do them, the less you have to do in crunch mode.

Week Before

- Obtain permit if your town requires one
- Get change/small bills
- Borrow tables from friends/family
- Any tasks you haven't completed from above list

3 Days Before

- Start advertising on internet (Craigslist, Facebook, etc.)
- Add dates and times to your signs
- Gather items you need to have on hand (see list on next page)
- Any tasks you haven't completed from above lists

2 Days Before

- Start setting up in a garage if possible (start 1 or 2 days earlier if you have a lot of stuff)
- Continue advertising on the internet

- E-mail all your friends and relatives telling them about the sale

1 Day Before

- Continue setting up and pricing everything
- Big burst of advertising all over the internet
- Bump up all your posts in Facebook groups
- Hang signs if no rain or heavy winds in the overnight forecast and you live in an area where you think your signs won't get stolen or taken down
- Verify you have all the things you need to have on hand for your sale (see list below)

Morning of Sale

- Hang signs if not done the day before
- Set up tables and free-standing shelves in yard or driveway if not already set up in a garage
- Cover all tables with cloths if you're going to
- Spread a tarp out if you're going to put things on the ground
- Cart all your stuff out to yard or driveway
- Set up all the smaller items on tables, shelves, or on a tarp

- Place a sign and any attention getter(s) at end of driveway
- Start selling!

Things to Have on Hand During Sale

- Tables
- Table coverings
- Something to put your money in (apron, fanny pack, cash box)
- Small bills and coins to make change – approximately 25 single dollar bills, 5-10 five dollar bills, 2-3 ten dollar bills, and at least $5 in coins
- Calculator
- Bags for customers' purchases recycled from previous shopping trips
- Newspaper or packing paper to wrap breakables
- Price tags and price stickers
- Pen, pencil, marker, and note paper
- Receipt book (in case anyone asks for a receipt)
- Clip board
- Empty boxes (that customers can fill)

- Scotch tape
- Masking tape
- Tape measure
- Easy access to electrical outlet or long extension cord to test electrical items
- Batteries to test electronics
- Sunscreen
- Paper Towels
- Food for you and your helpers (both lunch and dinner since you probably won't feel like cooking after your sale is over)

Chapter 5: Tips on Setting Up

If you have a garage or other indoor area where you are able to set up for the sale several days early, it will save you a lot of craziness the morning of your sale trying to set up outside while customers are swarming around. You'll still have plenty of setting up to do that morning, but whatever you can do ahead of time will help save your sanity the morning of the sale.

Ideally, you should have plenty of tables to use for your sale. If you borrow any from friends or family, make sure you tag them somehow with the name of the person you borrowed each one from so there is no mix-up when returning them to their owners.

If you don't have enough tables, you can use a piece of plywood or an old door placed across saw horses, then cover the top with some kind of table covering to make it look nice. If you have a picnic table in your backyard, move it to your front yard prior to the sale, and you can use both the table top and benches to put things on. A board placed across two dairy crates can also be used to put things on it. Get creative and make a table out of anything you have, just be sure it is secure enough so if anyone leans against it, it won't shift or collapse.

Shelves are also useful for displaying garage sale items. Shelves can be metal, wood, or plastic—any kind will work as long as they won't easily topple over and the items on them are easily visible.

If you have a garage where all your stuff is being stored for the sale--even if you're not actually holding the sale inside the garage---set up as many tables as possible with merchandise inside the garage the night before. Then the morning of the sale two people can lift and move the tables outside to your yard or driveway. This will help you set up quicker than if you have to load all your tables with merchandise the morning of your sale. Don't place glassware or other fragile items on any tables you are planning to move.

If you are holding the sale inside your garage, set up your "floor plan" first, putting up and positioning all your tables and shelves before loading anything on them. Keep in mind how the flow of traffic will work if the garage fills up with shoppers. You want to try to arrange your tables and shelves so there is enough room for shoppers to stop and look at things, while allowing enough room for other shoppers to get by them.

If you're holding the sale inside your garage, cover up anything that isn't for sale—bikes, lawn mowers, garbage cans, yard tools, etc. If it's not for sale, put it out of sight by covering it with an old sheet or blanket. If nothing else, rope off an area of the garage and put a large "Not For Sale" sign in front of that area. If stuff is roped off with a "Not For Sale" sign, it's pretty obvious, but you'll still get people who will ask if your lawn mower is for sale if they spot it in the back of the garage. For this reason, I prefer covering things up whenever possible.

Make Things Look Nice

How much time you have to set up may determine how nice you can make things look, but the nicer it looks, the more your merchandise will appeal to buyers.

As mentioned earlier, all dirty items should be cleaned ahead of time to make them more appealing to buyers. Cover all tables with cloths or fabric. Don't use anything with a busy pattern that will distract from the merchandise—instead, use a fabric that will make your merchandise stand out. Solid colors or very subtle patterns you can barely see are best. Dark color table coverings can make your display look rich, but it can also absorb your merchandise depending on what it is.

Sparkly jewelry or crystal glassware look great on a black fabric, but if you're selling items that are black or dark brown, they'll get lost on a black table covering. Most items stand out better on a light colored table covering, but if you are selling something like a bunch of white milk glass, you should put them on a table covering that will contrast nicely with it.

Covering your tables dresses up your merchandise and makes your sale look more interesting and more appealing than if your items are sitting on a dirty, beat-up table, or a bare piece of plywood. Table coverings don't have to be table cloths--you can also use bed sheets, blankets, curtains, or a large piece of fabric.

There are some instances where fluff doesn't matter. If you're selling things like tools or car parts, the "rustic" look on a bare piece of plywood is fine, but if you're selling jewelry, purses, vintage linens, or items that appeal more to women, you'll do better if you make them look pretty.

I mentioned earlier that you can sell pretty much anything at a garage sale, including broken, junky stuff. However, put the nicer stuff in the high visibility areas and the broken, junky stuff in less visible areas.

You don't want your customers coming in, seeing a bunch of broken, dirty items, and getting turned off. You want stuff at your sale to look nice, and if it does, people are willing to pay more for it.

If everything at your sale is dirty and piled on top of each other in boxes, your customers are going to expect rock-bottom prices. If your motivation for having the sale is just to get rid of everything and you don't care what you get for it, then by all means, leave everything as is, but plan to sell your items for low, low prices. If you hope to make as much as you can while getting rid of things, make it look attractive to buyers.

Make Things Easy To See

If you can get your hands on lightweight plastic shelves that you assemble yourself, you can increase your display area by placing the shelves on top of your tables. You can use either a single shelf or two shelves to have merchandise tiered at different eye levels for more visual appeal. Shelves on top of the table work only if the table is up against a wall in a garage or a house. Set up in a driveway or yard, a display like this wouldn't work effectively because you risk too much bumping or heavy winds knocking things off them. The last thing you want is the entire set of shelves and everything on it to come crashing down because a customer bumped the table. Inside, up against a wall, if the table is bumped, the wall behind it helps keep the shelves secure and strong wind blowing things off generally isn't a problem.

I purchased plastic shelves for my sales at bargain prices at thrift shops or other people's garage sales, but you can buy them new at any department store. They are versatile enough that you can probably find a use for them after your sale.

If possible, try to get boxes of items you want people to go through off the ground so it's easier for customers to go through them. A box of toys on the ground is great for kids to sit and pick through while their parents shop, but it's not so easy for people who can't squat or bend easily.

Having stuff on tables is usually better for your customers to see things than if you leave everything in boxes on the ground, but if you don't have enough tables for everything, you need to get creative to make those boxes easy to go through. I often use dairy crates with a board across them to create just enough of a riser so the buyer can pick out things in the boxes without bending or squatting to the ground. To make them look nicer, I hide the crates and board by covering them with a cloth. I've also placed boxes of merchandise on top of large plastic storage bins (covered with a cloth) to get them off the ground and closer to eye level. If your customers can't easily see something, they won't buy it. Make it as easy as possible for them to see things. If you see someone struggling to look through a box you have on the ground, offer to place it on top of a table, a chair or some other higher location to make it easier for them to go through it.

Jewelry should be bagged or displayed in a way that makes it appealing and easy to see. Don't put it all in a jewelry box that people have to hunt through to find mates for earrings, or deal with a big pile of necklaces or bracelets that got tangled up as shoppers rummaged through them. Ideally have jewelry located close to where you will be most of the time as it's one of the most likely items to "walk away."

A collapsible clothing rack works well for displaying linens. Be sure to put a sign "Rack not for sale" if you're not selling it. If you are trying to sell the rack, loading it up with stuff isn't the best way to get rid of it because it won't get seen. You're better off leaving the rack clutter free if you want to get rid of it, or just put one or two small items on it so the rack is still pretty visible. Be sure to put a visible price tag on it, or better yet a sign that says "Clothing rack" along with the price.

People are more likely to look at clothing that is hanging up than they are to dig through a jumbled mess of clothes in a box. If you have a portable clothing rack, hang all your nicest items on it. You can hang clothing from a clothesline or strong rope tied between two trees, or if you have a fence nearby, put clothing on hangers all along the length of it. You can hang clothing from a porch railing, or create a makeshift clothing rack by placing a metal pole between two ladders and securely anchoring it so it doesn't shift.

While hanging all your clothes is the best way to have them easily seen by customers, putting your clothing on a table is second best. Clothing that is folded neatly may look appealing first thing in the morning, but unfortunately, clothing never stays folded for long. Many people won't bother folding something back up after they look at it, so unless you don't mind folding clothing all day long in an attempt to keep it orderly, you might as well just spread clothes out in neat piles on the table. Arrange them so that each category of clothing has their own pile--all the jeans together, all the tee-shirts together, etc. Clothes are easier to see on a table than in a box, so if you can't hang them and you have enough table space, use it for your clothes.

If you are selling books, put them in boxes with the spines up and all the titles going in the same direction so customers can easily see all the titles at a glance. If books are randomly piled in boxes, it is more difficult for customers in a hurry to go through them. Books with spines up works best for thicker books. Thinner books such as children's soft or hardcovers are better displayed upright in a box so people can flip through them easily. If you can get those boxes of books off the ground somehow, it will make it that much easier for people to go through.

Adequate lighting is a must if you hold your sale inside a garage or other indoor area. Anyone coming in from the bright outdoors may have trouble seeing when they first come in, and even after their eyes adjust, your garage might be too dark for them to see merchandise clearly. If your garage tends to be dark, set up extra lighting so that your customers can easily see your merchandise. Floor lamps, shop lights that can be hung from rafters, or free-standing flood lights won't use up valuable table space and are good candidates for auxiliary lights. Just be sure to mark whatever light you are using with a sign "Light not for sale," unless, of course, you are selling it too.

The best way to get customers to buy your stuff is to make sure everything is easy to see, easy to access, and easy to go through.

Put Like Things Together

When setting things up, I prefer to put like things together. If I am selling a lot of model cars or lots of toys, I always put them in the same area so they are easier to spot for anyone looking for them. If you put all your ceramic figurines together, someone who like ceramic figurines will immediate gravitate towards where they are. If you have half a dozen old dolls you're selling, display them together rather than scattered around the yard or garage and doll lovers will most likely head to that area first. Where the dolls are is where you should also put any doll clothing, doll cases, doll stands, or anything else doll related that you are selling.

There is a downside to having a lot of the same thing together. While a whole table of green glassware might look appealing to a die-hard green glassware collector, for some people it is overwhelming to pick out just one when there are so many to choose from. If there was only one piece of green glass, they might buy it thinking it's unique or rare (plus it's the only one and they have to have it!), but if you have a dozen similar pieces, people might feel it's pretty common stuff and pass it all up. In cases like this, sometimes less is better.

The way I deal with having too much of something is to put out only a few pieces and if they sell, I put out more or tell people when they're paying for them, that I have more if they are interested. For me, this works because I have enough garage sales that I know if I can't sell something at one sale, I'll sell it at my next one. For you, if you don't want to hang on to anything for another sale, you'll probably want to put everything out all at once to try to get rid of it.

If you have a lot of similar items, try putting only a few of them on the table, and the rest under the table. If someone shows interest in the ones on the table, you can always point out the others tucked underneath.

Chapter 6: Day of the Sale

Morning Set Up

All your hard work leading up to the sale will come to
a full head the morning of the sale. Make sure you give
yourself plenty of time for setting up, even if you had
the benefit of setting a lot of your stuff up early inside
a garage. How long you'll need depends on how much
stuff you still have to set up or drag out to the yard
and how much help you have.

You should give yourself at least an hour, but if you
have a lot of stuff and didn't do any pre-setting up,
you might need two hours—especially if you have to
hang signs too. Keep in mind, early birds—especially
dealers--often show up anywhere from an hour to a
half hour before a sale starts. As your start time draws

closer, more early birds will be swopping in. The less time you give yourself for setting up, the more you'll be dealing with these early shoppers getting in your way. Even if you're having a small sale with only a few tables worth of stuff, it's better to set up early and sit around for a half hour waiting for customers to come than to deal with the craziness that can happen if you start setting up too close to your opening time.

If you didn't hang signs the day before, put them up first thing, even before setting up. Ideally, it would be nice if you have one or two people putting up signs while a couple of other people start setting up for the sale, but if you're doing it all yourself, start with the signs first as you shouldn't leave your sale once it's set up.

Attention Getters

If your sale is out of sight from the road, say it's held in a garage at the end of a long driveway, you need to make sure people know you're there. Have something big, shiny, or colorful that people can't miss at the end of your driveway—perhaps a giant stuffed animal, a kid's playhouse, or a bouquet of balloons—along with a large garage sale sign. Having several large items leading down the driveway helps draw attention to where you have the bulk of your stuff set up. I've driven right past sales that I couldn't see because everything was inside a garage that wasn't visible from the direction I was coming from. Only by backtracking did I find the sale. Make sure cars coming from any direction will know there's a sale on.

Most people holding sales don't bother putting a sign at the end of the driveway because they figure it's obvious they're having a sale, and no sign is needed. However, if your sale is down the end of a long driveway, inside a house or garage, in your back yard, or anywhere the sale isn't easily visible, it's important to put a sign by the road with an arrow pointing the way. A sign at the end of your driveway leaves no question where the sale is. It's the fear of many garage salers that they'll unintentionally go into garages of people who are just cleaning theirs out or in the yard of someone who's moving and has all their belongings about to be loaded into a moving van, so help put those fears to rest with a big sign that lets everyone know you're definitely having a sale.

Wait until you're mostly set up to put the last sign at the end of your road or driveway. This might cut down on some early birds while you're still setting up. I find as soon as I put the sign at the end of my road, customers start coming, but it depends what kind of road you live on whether or not this will make a difference.

Dealing With Early Birds

Dealers, collectors, and die-hard yard salers will come early even if you say "no early birds" in all your ads. Garage salers who are out early will see your signs and come regardless of what time you open. You definitely shouldn't waste space on your signs saying "no early birds" because drivers won't have time to read that, plus see what your starting time is, then check to see what the current time it is before they zoom in the direction the arrow on your sign is pointing.

I've seen sellers who requested no early birds standing firm on it. If you are holding your sale indoors or in a garage, there's nothing wrong with waiting until your starting time to open the door to buyers. However, if you're having your sale in a yard, it's hard to keep early birds out unless your yard is fenced in and you keep the gate locked. I once watched in horror and fascination as a seller actually yelled at early customers to wait at the end of his driveway until the sale's start time. As they inched closer to try to look at stuff in his yard, he kept yelling at them to get back, that he wasn't open yet. Many people got back in their cars and drove away after witnessing how unpleasant the seller was. I was one of them.

Even if you requested no early birds in your ads, be prepared for them, and rather than get angry that they ignored your request, you're better off if you greet them with a smile and let them look. They may turn out to be your biggest customer of the day, so go with it.

I see novice sellers starting to set up their sales only half an hour before their opening time and the early birds are already there rifling through every box as the sellers brings new stuff out. Those sellers get overwhelmed trying to set up when people are asking them questions about prices and trying to make deals on stuff. While they're trying to answer questions, taking money from people, and still trying to set up, more people are coming by the minute. Try to avoid this scenario by (a) giving yourself plenty of time for setting up and (b) have plenty of help on hand so you can designate some people to help early customers and others to do the setting up. If you have enough people helping, designate someone to be a "security" person to stand off to the side and watch to try to make sure no one walks off without paying for something.

The early morning chaos is the time you need to be extra careful with mistakes being made where you give too much cash back, add up things wrong, or forget to take the money from someone. When three or four people are waving money at you, and others are asking how much you want for something, it's easy to make mistakes. Also, this is the worst time to leave your purse or cash box unguarded, even for a second, because with all the distractions, that money could walk away with someone.

Be Friendly and Helpful

Greet people, offer them help, but don't over-do it. I hate pushy salespeople and this includes at yard sales. I want to look without feeling pressured to buy something. I think most people feel the same way. I tend to start feeling uncomfortable if the person running the sale is watching my every move and every time I pick up anything they try to convince me how great the item is in case I couldn't see that for myself or tell me they'll give me a good price for it, or tell me how the item came from Pottery Barn to justify why they have it priced so high. The more a seller does this, the more I want to be left alone by them. That being said, if someone seems interested in something at your sale, you certainly can talk it up, tell them the history, tell them how it works, or tell them you can do better on the price. Just don't do that for every item the person looks at. Save the sales talk for those items where someone looks like they are seriously thinking about buying it, but can't decide.

Talking up your merchandise does pay off, when played gently. Sometimes people need help or a little nudge to decide whether to buy something. By all means, engage with them, talk about the assets of the item, be friendly, be helpful, but also know when to step back and just let people shop on their own.

While you're being friendly and engaging with one customer, try not to ignore all the others. If you are chatting away with one customer, another may get frustrated and leave instead of waiting for you to be free to ask a question about something they are interested in. Always keep an eye out for anyone looking for assistance and if you're involved with one customer, excuse yourself for a moment to see if the other person's question is quick, or let know they'll be next to be helped. By acknowledging them instead of ignoring them, they're more likely to wait for you to be free. Also, if you are standing around chatting with a customer or a neighbor that stopped by, try not to block your tables or stand in front of items other customers might want to look at. Try to move the conversation over to an area that won't block people from seeing your merchandise.

In the event your sale slows up and you are passing the time talking on the phone with a friend, hang up if a customer comes. You wouldn't like it if you walked into a store and the cashier was yakking away on her cell phone the whole time she rang up your order, so don't do the same to your customers. As soon as a car pulls up in front of your house, get off your phone and be available to welcome and help the person who is coming to your sale.

All Items Should Be Paid In Full

My first experience with running a moving sale was when I was 13 years old helping my two teenage sisters get rid of a house full of stuff. We learned a hard lesson from that first moving sale when we allowed a customer to cart off a truck full of furniture without paying for it. We hadn't asked for the money for the furniture before allowing him to load it all on his truck, and only after the heavy pieces were already loaded in the truck did he tell us that he didn't have the money on him to pay for it. He promised he'd go home, get the money, and he'd be right back. Naïve as we were, we said, "Okay." That guy got himself a beautiful set of furniture for free because he never came back to pay for it.

Perhaps the guy really was honest and he just couldn't remember the way back to our house to pay us, or maybe he knew exactly what he was doing and was laughing all the way home at the three dumb kids he just ripped off, but learn from mine and my sisters' experience---always have the money in hand before releasing the goods.

I've heard similar stories from a number of other people who had items taken from their sales without being paid for. They've helped customers load their cars with items, spent some time chatting with them all nice and friendly, and only after the people drove off, did they realize no money had exchanged hands for those items. You don't want something like this to happen to you, so don't be shy about asking for payment first before you help anyone load their car with stuff.

If someone doesn't have enough money to pay for something and asks you to hold it while they run to the nearest ATM, ask them to put down a deposit so you know they are serious about coming back for it. How much of a deposit to ask for depends on the price of the item, but make it significant enough that they'll come back. Tell them you'll hold the item for twenty minutes while they get the rest of the money, and if they're not back after twenty minutes, it goes back up for sale. You can always return their deposit if it sells to someone else before they get back, but you should at least honor the agreed upon hold time. Obviously, you can wait longer than twenty minutes if you'd like, but the less time you give them, the faster they'll hurry back. You shouldn't promise to hold something for more than half an hour for anyone unless you know them and know they will follow through.

If you promise to hold an item for an hour or more, or without specifying exactly when they need to be back, the person could come back hours later and say they changed their mind and want their deposit back. You've then missed out on other potential buyers who may have been interested in the item during that time, and possibly missed your opportunity of selling it at all that day. If anyone needs more than half an hour to get money to pay for something, tell them they'll have to take a chance that it will still be there when they come back. If they want an item bad enough, they'll figure out a way to get the money quickly and get back to your sale before the item is gone.

Be Ready to Negotiate Prices

It's a given that yard sale prices are negotiable. Yes, you can stay firm on some things, but if you refuse to budge on any of your prices, you're going to end up *not* selling a lot of stuff. Most people like to price things higher than what they want for something so that there is some room to come down. This is fine, but if you price it too high, it's going to turn people off right from the start. Some people will figure the price is already out of their negotiation range so won't even bother making an offer.

If you're pricing things higher than what you'd like to get for it so that you can come down, then price it only a little higher. If you want $25 for something, pricing it at $50 will scare off a lot of customers. If you price it at $30-$35, then people are going to assume you'll be able to come down to $25 and they'll offer you that. Some people who know your item is worth more than $35 might pay that price without any haggling, but most will ask if you can come down. If you have an item that you want good money for and you'd rather keep the item if you can't get a decent price for it, go ahead and price it high. Just be prepared to keep the item if no one is willing to pay your asking price.

Sometimes I'll price my items at the lowest price I'm willing to take for an item and when a customer ask for a lower price, I'll explain that it's already priced low for a quick sale. Or I'll explain that I just lowered the price and I tell them what I originally was asking for it. Sometimes the person ends up buying it at my asking price, but occasionally I'll have persistent customers who keep insisting I go lower. Depending on how badly I want to get rid of something I might bend and go even lower, but other times I stand firm on my price.

It's always a gamble when to haggle and when to stand firm, but if you're friendly and nice while the haggling is going on rather than acting insulted or angry about low offers, you'll get more sales. Some people will make insulting low-ball offers on some things, but instead of telling them where they can stuff their offer, just smile politely and say, "Thank you but that's much lower than I'm willing to go."

Keeping Things Fresh

During my sale, I tend to move stuff around as the day goes on. If I find people are gravitating to a certain area of my sale and, for whatever reason, that area is a hot spot for selling things, I'll keep moving more items to that area every time something gets sold. I also like to keep rearranging items so my sale never looks picked over with big empty spots. If people come and see a lot of empty tables, they'll assume all the good stuff is gone. Move stuff around to fill in empty spots on tables, or remove tables altogether if you've gotten rid of a lot of stuff.

Security

Warning: Some of your merchandise may get stolen at your sale. It doesn't always happen, but sometimes it does. Some people who have yard sales might not care if someone walks off with an item or two without paying for it because it's stuff they wanted to get rid of anyway. If you're not one of those people and you do care—make sure you have a helper with you who can keep an eye on things while you're helping other customers. As much as we'd like to think no one would do something like that where we live, no matter where you live, there are people who will take what's not rightfully theirs.

Most people who steal from yard sales take merchandise, but sometimes they steal cash too. I know someone who had all her cash stolen when she got distracted at a sale. There will be plenty of distractions during your sale, so you need to be sure your money is always in a secure place. At one sale I attended, I opened a box sitting on a table with merchandise and found it was loaded with cash. The box was what the seller was using to hold her money from the sale, and she set it down on the table for a moment then forgot about it when she got distracted.

The same thing happened at another sale I went to. There sitting among the merchandise was a small box holding the seller's money. If I wasn't an honest person, both those times I could have easily grabbed a handful of money out of the box and the seller would have never missed it. More times than I can count, I've seen customers ask a question about something and watched as the seller walked over to them, leaving their cash box sitting unguarded.

A cash box is not the best place to keep your money during your yard sale unless you have plenty of people helping you with the sale and you or one of your trusted helpers is keeping one hand on it at all times. If you do use one and you're working alone, when you get up, take your cash box with you and never put it down to work on something. No one wants to go through the hard work of hosting a yard sale only to have some thief run off with all their money. Many people are honest enough and they wouldn't take a box of cash if they saw it unguarded, but it only takes one dishonest person and there goes your profits for all your hard work.

Rather than a money box, it's safer to keep your money on you. This way, if you're running around a lot during a sale you don't unintentionally leave it sitting unguarded. Keep your money in an apron with deep pockets, in a fanny pack (they aren't stylish, but they work!), in a money holder attached securely, or in your pants pocket if they are deep enough.

I usually keep my bills in a money holder around my waist. As the day goes on, I remove any bills I have a lot of as well as all but a few $20 bills since I probably won't use too many to make change. I take that money and put it in the house. This way my cash wad doesn't get too thick or unmanageable, plus I'm not carrying it all if something should happen to it. My coins, which tend to get too heavy for me to cart around all day, I keep in a small container hidden out of sight and in an area off limits to customers. I rarely keep more than $5 in it. If the coin container gets too full, I take the excess into the house for safekeeping as well. Even if someone found and stole my small hoard of coins, they'd only get about $5.

Since we're on the subject of stealing, if you are running a sale by yourself or it's just you and your spouse working the sale and no one's in the house, keep your house locked up. If you're both distracted— maybe helping someone carry something to their car—someone else could sneak into your house and help themselves to your valuables. Sad but true, this has happened to people running sales.

It never hurts to take some precautions before and during your sale to help protect your sales money, your merchandise, and your home.

Chapter 7: Last Day of Sale

If you've held a two- or three-day sale and you still have a lot of items left over the last day, you might want to consider dropping your prices. Put up signs indicating "everything negotiable," or "50% off all marked prices." You'll especially want to lower the price on all the big items in order to get rid of them. Hopefully, you sold enough stuff the first day that whatever you get the second or third day is icing on the cake. Even if you didn't make as much or get rid of as much as you hoped the first day or two, the last day should still be the bargain day so you don't have as much to donate, toss, or put back into storage.

As the day goes on and you're still left with items that almost no one showed interest in the previous day(s) of your sale, you might want to consider just giving it away--especially if you only have an hour or two left until closing time. Put items you don't want to keep that you don't think anyone is going to buy at the end of your driveway with a free sign and hope someone coming late to your sale takes it away and saves you the hassle of doing it. You can also post a photo of all your freebies in your Facebook yard sale groups and let people know the stuff is there for the taking for the next hour or two. Maybe you'll get a few last minute customers who will come for the freebies, but end up buying some stuff as well. If you still have something left that has value and you don't want to just give it away, photograph it while it's outside and plan to try to sell it later on Craigslist.

Cleaning Up

Ideally, by the end of your sale you've sold everything and there is nothing left to put away, right? Yeah, right! After all the years I've been doing sales, this has never happened to me, but maybe you'll get lucky and it will happen for you. Even if it doesn't, hopefully, there will be a lot less stuff to deal with at the end of the sale then there was at the beginning. Since I have a large garage, at the end of the last day I just drag everything that is left in the driveway into the garage and close the door to deal with it the next day when I have more energy. If you don't have the luxury of a garage to postpone the clean up for another day or you have to work the next day and won't have time, then you'll need to deal with what's left right away. Hopefully, you'll have plenty of help with the cleanup, and you can get it done quickly.

As you are packing up stuff at the end of the sale, you need to decide which items to keep, donate, or toss. Box or bag up all the stuff you want to donate, and clearly write "Donate" on every box or tape a note on every bag going to a thrift shop or charity. If possible, load anything being donated directly in your car so you can take them the following day. You can also arrange to have a nonprofit organization come and pick up donated goods directly from your house. You can find a list of charities and areas where they pick up at http://donationtown.org/donation-pick-up.html. Anything you want to keep, bring back into your house, and anything not worth donating or keeping, throw out.

You should always take down all your signs after your sale—usually the same day it ends or at the very latest, the next morning. Taking down your signs is a courtesy to everyone, including to die-hard garage salers who might end up looking at your signs the following weekend and come to your house looking for a sale that's long over. Since your address is usually on signs it's also a smart thing to remove them so you don't get fined for leaving them up or for littering if they fall down.

After the unsold stuff is put away and your signs are down, it's time to count the wad of money you made and enjoy the extra space you've gained from all the stuff you sold.

Chapter 8: Having Additional Sales

If you made tons of money running a sale, don't expect to be as profitable if you decide to do a second sale a couple weeks later to try to get rid of more stuff. Many regular yard salers don't like to go to sales that are held a second or even a third time. They figure everything is already picked over and you're selling the leftovers. Even if you advertise "all new stuff" you might not be as successful having a second sale as you were with the first sale if you have them too close together. Those sellers who open their garage door weekend after weekend and try to sell the same items will find the number of customers who come will go down every time they open. One of the few exceptions to this might be someone who lives in a high traffic area of a tourist spot where there are many new people driving by their sale every week.

If you need to have more than one sale because you still have lots of stuff you want to get rid of, you need to (a) wait a decent amount of time between sales— say do one in May and again in September, or (b) try to hold your second sale in a different location—at a friend's or relative's house where hopefully you'll get a lot of different customers or (c) capitalize on a big event happening nearby that is bound to bring in a lot of people—including a whole host of die-hard garage sale lovers who might not have gone to your first sale.

That being said, having two back-to-back garage sales means most of the work for the second one has already been done, so it might be an easy way to make a few more dollars and get rid of a few more things. Also, if your first sale was a bust because of rain or 104 degree heat that kept people inside all day, by all means try it again the following weekend if sunny skies are predicted or the heat index isn't going to frighten people off. Just remember to advertise it just as much (or more) than you did the first time and don't skimp on the sign hanging.

End Note

After having a bad garage or yard sale, many people are gun-shy about ever having another. I can't count the number of people who have sworn to me that they will never do another sale because it wasn't worth the effort for the little bit of money they made when they did one.

If you ran a sale and it didn't do so well, the best thing to do is give it another go. Don't let a bad sale keep you from trying again. Try to figure out why your last sale wasn't good. Was it because you didn't get enough customers? Then you need to figure out how to get more people to come to your next sale (advertise, advertise, advertise). Was it because the people who came didn't buy? Then you need to figure out if you had the right stuff to sell, if your prices were competitive enough (as in low enough for customers to want to buy, but high enough so you made something), or whether you were advertising in the right places to bring in the right people for the stuff you were selling. Was it because the weather worked against you? Then try to plan another day when the weather looks like it will be good. Was it because you were competing with too many other sales in the area? Then try to hold your next sale when there aren't so many—maybe start your sale a day ahead of when most of the other sales start. Did it seem like you got rid of a lot of stuff, but still made no money? Then your next sale you need to be sure you have some higher dollar items (but still bargained priced to sell) to help give your profits a boost.

Like any job, running a garage or yard sale does require a good deal of effort in order to be successful. You can't just do the minimum amount of work you can get away with, then expect to do well. While it can happen, the odds are better that it won't.

If you're willing to educate yourself on ways to make your sale successful, and you're willing to work hard to make it happen, then your next sale will be better than your last one. While obviously there are some factors you have no control over that might work against you, how much pre-planning, preparation, and advertising you do, along with realistic pricing and providing friendly and helpful customer service can make a huge difference on your profits. If you implement many of the tips found in this book, you'll increase your odds of making your next sale a good one.

Thank you for reading <u>The Garage Sale How-To Guide</u>. If you found this book helpful, please be sure to recommend it to your friends and share a review of it on Amazon and Goodreads. If there is anything you'd like to see added or changed for future versions, you can e-mail me through one of my websites listed on the following page.

About the Author

Cindy Sabulis was introduced to yard sales as a young teen when she and her sisters held a moving sale on the front porch of their home. There she got her first lesson on what *not* to do when holding a sale. As an adult, she continued making newbie mistakes when running garage sales, but as her ignorance lessened, her profits rose. Over the next three decades she perfected her garage-sale-holding skills, with each sale getting bigger and better than the previous one. In addition to running her own sales, she is a sucker for helping friends and relatives run theirs. By applying the methods she discusses in this book, she helps ensure every sale is successful.

Cindy is a writer of both fiction and nonfiction, and is the owner of Toys of Another Time, a company which specializes in selling vintage dolls and toys. Her published books are available through her websites and many other online sources. Cindy's writing site is at www.cindysabulis.com and her vintage collectibles website is at www.toysofanothertime.com.

34500448R00071

Made in the USA
Middletown, DE
23 August 2016